MAD®

THE COMPLETE HALF-WIT AND WISDOM OF

ALFRED E. NEUMAN

FALL RIVER PRESS

New York

FALL RIVER PRESS

New York

An Imprint of Sterling Publishing
387 Park Avenue South
New York, NY 10016

This 2014 compilation published by Fall River Press.

Contents of this compilation appeared originally in slightly different form in *The Half-Wit and Wisdom of Alfred E. Neuman* and *MAD Neumanisms: More Half-Wit and Wisdom of Alfred E. Neuman.*

ISBN 978-1-4351-5559-6

Distributed in Canada by Sterling Publishing
c/o Canadian Manda Group, 165 Dufferin Street
Toronto, Ontario, Canada M6K 3H6

For information about custom editions, special sales, and premium and corporate purchases,
please contact Sterling Special Sales at 800-805-5489 or specialsales@sterlingpublishing.com.

Manufactured in the United States of America

2 4 6 8 10 9 7 5 3 1

www.sterlingpublishing.com

Visit MAD online at www.madmagazine.com

Though Alfred E. Neuman wasn't the first to say, "A fool and his money are soon parted," here's your chance to prove the old adage right-subscribe to MAD! Simply call 1-800-4-MADMAG and mention code 5MBN2. Operators are standing by (the water cooler).

Contents

Words to Live By

It's a good idea to keep your words soft and sweet because you never know when you'll have to eat them.

Smoking helps you lose weight—
one lung at a time.

If you live each day as if it were your last, you'll be filled with tubes and coughing up blood!

Experience is what makes you pause briefly before going ahead and making the same mistake.

Every dog has its day—but in dog years that's like a whole week!

PEARL OF IDIOCY

Live every day as if it were your last, because one of these days you'll be right!

After all is said and done, there's always a lot more said than done!

There's more than one way to skin a cat, though you probably won't even need the one.

In retrospect, it becomes clear that hindsight is definitely overrated.

You'll never get rid of a bad temper by losing it!

When you're in deep water
it's a good idea to keep
your mouth shut!

On their deathbed, no one ever wished they had spent more time at the office—or on their deathbed, for that matter!

If we really learned from our past mistakes, most of us would never get out of bed in the morning.

It's better to sleep on
something you plan
to do than to be kept
awake by something
you've done.

When it comes to personal conduct, always set the bar high—it makes it much easier to sneak underneath!

There is more poetry in the simple song of a bird than in any ten symphonies, except all the poetry tends to be about worms.

Experience is something you never have until just after you need it.

Life is what happens to you while you're busy making future plans.

PEARL OF IDIOCY

Every dog has its day—but that day still consists largely of sniffing butts.

At one time or another, everybody plays the fool—but some people are typecast for life!

Be wary of anyone who gives you advice that begins with "Be wary of . . ."

In the land of the blind, the one-eyed man is king. There are also very few archery contests.

Understatement is a zillion times more effective than exaggeration!

Many a good egg ends up getting beaten!

Success is achieved only by those who are more or less confident, kind of specific, and take a relatively firm stand.

If at first you don't succeed . . . you're about normal.

PEARL OF IDIOCY

Man cannot live on bread alone . . . but plenty get by on just the crust!

Politics and Government

The problem with the economy is that our budget is balanced by people who aren't!

Many an election is won by the candidate who can fake sincerity better.

PEARL OF IDIOCY

Anyone who says the truth shall set you free has never been to traffic court!

It's astonishing how politicians never say anything, yet always insist they're being misquoted.

America is the land that fought for freedom and then began passing laws to get rid of it.

War is what happens when arms are used instead of heads!

Too many politicians who wave the flag want to waive what it stands for.

Political campaign speeches are like steer horns: a point here, a point there . . . and a lot of bull in between!

Have you noticed that political promises are usually in one year and out the other?

These days, the only time politicians are telling the truth is when they call each other a liar.

It's no wonder politicians don't listen to their conscience. They don't want to take advice from a total stranger.

The reason politicians are so busy is that they spend half their time passing laws and the other half helping their friends get around them.

Ever notice how many government officials make their raises effective long before *they* ever are?

Remember the good old days, when the government lived within its income and without most of yours?

The ups and downs of the economy are the result of having elected too many yo-yos!

Isn't it amazing how political candidates can give you all their good points and qualifications in a thirty-second TV commercial?

Elections are when people find out what politicians stand for and politicians find out what people will fall for.

People

If most people said what's on their minds, they'd be speechless.

Germs attack people where they're weakest—which is why there are so many head colds.

A masochist is one who paints himself into a corner and then applies a second coat.

People who live in glass houses ... are a reality TV producer's dream come true.

Men who will eat only their mother's cooking have an edible complex.

The reason most people talk to themselves is because they're often the only ones who will listen!

A bore is somebody who interrupts your fifth story with one of his own.

A call girl is a lady who isn't free for the night.

People with bad coughs
should go to doctors
instead of theaters.

PEARL OF IDIOCY

Modesty is the art of drawing attention to whatever it is you're being humble about.

A lot of people who complain they don't get what they deserve don't know how lucky they are.

People on ego trips should buy one-way tickets.

M ost people are so lazy, they don't even exercise good judgment.

Even the man who has everything is envious of the man who has two of everything.

Usually, when people give up smoking, they substitute something else for it . . . mainly bragging.

Most people who ask for a minute of your time have trouble timing a minute.

Genius is rarely recognized in its lifetime, but fortunately, neither is gross incompetence.

There was a time when a preacher's Little Black Book was a Bible!

When most people put in their two cents' worth, they are not overcharging.

Ever notice how people who say, "That's the way the ball bounces," are usually the ones who dropped it?

Most people don't mind a hard day's work— just as long as they're not in that day!

Too often, people who want
to offer sound advice give
us more sound than advice.

PEARL OF IDIOCY

Good hospitality is making your guests feel at home, even when you wish they were!

A couch potato follows the
path of least existence.

It's not just the ups and downs that make life difficult, it's the jerks.

You never know how many friends you have until you own a summer place!

PEARL OF IDIOCY

Vision is what some people claim they have when they find that they've guessed correctly.

Most of us don't know exactly what we want, but we're pretty sure we don't have it.

People who live in glass houses . . . should look like Sharon Stone!

PEARL OF IDIOCY

How is it that people looking for a helping hand tend to overlook the one at the end of their arm?

Put 1,000 writers in a room for 1,000 days and one will come up with a story about monkeys writing *Hamlet*!

Some minds are like concrete . . . all mixed up and permanently set.

The reason most people are lost in thought is because it's unfamiliar territory.

Most people don't act stupid—it's the real thing!

Ever notice that to entertain some people all you have to do is listen?

An argument is two people trying to get the last word in first!

If people wanted your unsolicited advice, they'd ask for it!

Modern Life

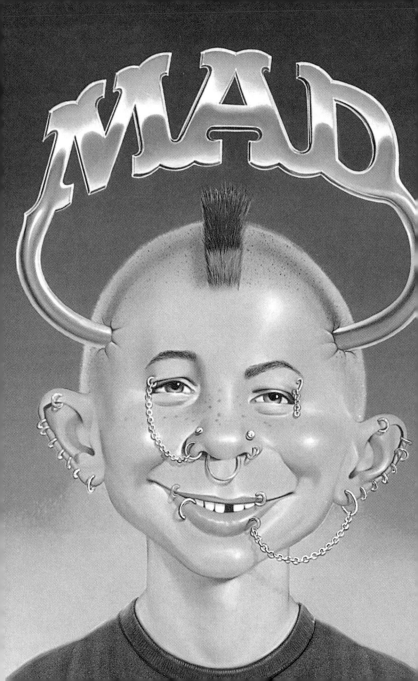

We're living in an age when lemonade is made with artificial ingredients and furniture polish is made with real lemons.

The suburbs are where they cut down all the trees and then name the streets after them.

Only in America could a letter that offers a prize of ten million dollars be regarded as junk mail.

Nuclear energy may be one thing that will finally prove to us that all men are cremated equal.

Prison inmates are treated to cable TV, hot meals, and a college education, while on the outside some people can afford these things only through a life of crime.

Thanks to the welfare bill, the question "Paper or plastic?" now refers to many Americans' sleeping arrangements.

Too many movies today have a beginning, a muddle, and an end.

Life is like a shower: one wrong turn and you're in hot water!

In Hollywood these days, *what's* coming out isn't as interesting as *who's* coming out!

Astronomers point out that the universe is racing away from the Earth at 15,000 miles per second. Can you blame it?

PEARL OF IDIOCY

The great advantage of compact cars is that you can get twice as many of them into traffic jams.

The clearest digital signal is still flipping someone the bird.

Americans are the only people looking for a shortcut to the quick fix.

The trouble with most neighborhoods is that there are too many hoods in them, and not enough neighbors.

Blessed are the censors, for they shall inhibit the Earth.

A supermarket is where you spend half an hour hunting for instant coffee!

You know the world's in trouble when it takes 2,000 laws just to enforce the Ten Commandments!

Today's "non-conformists" are getting harder and harder to tell apart.

The trouble with modern apartments is: the walls are too thin when you try to sleep, and too thick when you try to listen.

Sex, Dating, and Love

A man will go out with a woman if she's really different from other women . . . the difference being she'll go out with him.

Notice how women who claim that all men are alike seldom have trouble spotting the difference between you and Tom Cruise?

The first thing a man notices about a woman . . . depends on which way she's going!

A wedding ring is like a tourniquet—it cuts off your circulation!

A kiss is valid proof that two heads are better than one.

Marriage and Family

Y ou can't hurry love—
but you can move up the
wedding to accommodate the
baby's arrival!

Parents treat their kids like teeth—they try bonding only once irreparable damage has been done!

A family vacation is when you go away with people you need to get away from.

Adam was lucky! He never had to listen to Eve talk about the other men she could have married.

Adolescence is that period in a child's life when parents become most difficult!

Marriage is like a bath: once you're into it and you're used to it, it's not so hot.

Raising children is like taking pictures: you never know how they'll come out!

Marriage is like drugs to some people: they keep taking one kind of dope after another.

Most wives are like ventriloquists—
they stand there nodding
while the dummy does
all the talking!

Parents are the ones who are there when you want to be alone with a date and nowhere to be found when you need five bucks.

Parents work so they can give their children a better life than they had—and then complain how easy their kids have it!

You can't go home again. At least that's what your parents will tell you on graduation day!

With current divorce rates, it seems that oftentimes the honeymoon is over before the honeymoon is over!

Money

When money talks nobody criticizes its accent!

Why is it that things always look greener in the other guy's wallet?

Your money and your vacation never seem to run out at the same time.

Sometimes, the best scheme for doubling your money is to fold it in half and stuff it back in your wallet.

These days, most people's bank accounts need month-to-month resuscitation!

A shepherd with no flock falls asleep counting creditors.

Too many people think the best way to get a leg up on their finances is to look for a handout.

The dollar will never fall as low as what some people will do to get it!

PEARL OF IDIOCY

Most people get into financial difficulty when they don't act their wage.

When you give back all your ill-gotten gains, you're a reformed crook. When you keep most of the loot and only give back a small part of it, you're a philanthropist.

It's called take-home pay because there's nowhere else you can go with it!

Misers are tough to live with, but they make terrific ancestors!

Living on a budget is the same as living beyond your means, except that now you have a record of it.

Today, money still talks. Trouble is you have to increase the volume a lot!

Ever notice how random chance always picks you for jury duty, but never to win the lottery?

Business

A born executive is
someone whose
father owns the business.

A successful person is a clod like you who worked harder.

PEARL OF IDIOCY

An employer is someone who's late when you're early and early when you're late.

For many bosses, "affirmative action" means hiring more yes-men.

A lawyer is someone who writes an eighty-page document and calls it a brief.

The early bird gets the worm . . . but look what happens to the early worm!

It's not the work that keeps most people from volunteering, it's the pay.

There's no business like show business, although in terms of compassion, the Mafia comes close.

Whoever said, "Talk is cheap" never dialed a 1-900 number!

All lawyers are cut from the same cloth—fleece!

Today, if you ask a car dealer to let you see something for ten grand, he'll show you the door.

Some people are like blisters: they show up right after the work is done.

The problem with the ladder of success is that by the time you've climbed it, you're considered over the hill!

It's really amazing how unimportant your job is when you ask for a raise . . . and how important it is when you want a day off.

As you get older, work seems a lot less fun, and fun seems a lot more work!

Remember—the Post Office will not deliver mail without postage. And sometimes, even with!

A judge is nothing
more than a lawyer
who's been benched.

Telephone psychics are better at making fortunes than reading them.

Nepotism is when the corporate ladder is built from the lumber of your family tree.

The big guns in business are those who haven't as yet been fired!

Most people are too lazy to open the door when opportunity knocks.

Before arguing with your boss, it may be well to look at both sides: their side . . . and the outside.

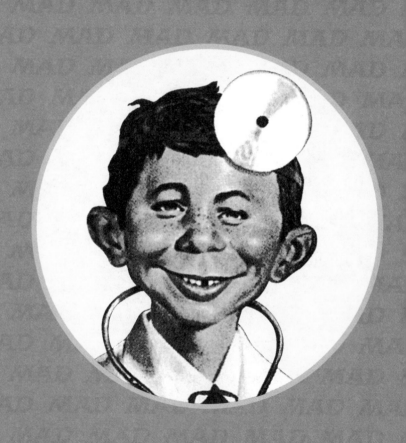

Doctors and Medicine

A psychiatrist is someone who hopefully finds out what makes a person tick before they explode!

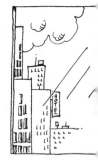

Before HMOs, medical insurance was what allowed people to be ill at ease.

The most troublesome side effect of many prescription drugs is that they make you feel well enough to go back to work.

Most doctors' gains are ill gotten!

The psychiatrist's office is where you say what you think and are told what you mean.

Any dentist who says, "This won't hurt a bit" is lying through your teeth!

If medicine isn't an exact science, how come they always know exactly how much to charge you?

What—me
Wworry?